Sweet TWEETS

SIMPLE STITCHES, WHIMSICAL BIRDS

Erin Cox

Martingale®
Create with Confidence

Sweet Tweets: Simple Stitches, Whimsical Birds
© 2015 by Erin Cox

Martingale®
19021 120th Ave. NE, Ste. 102
Bothell, WA 98011-9511 USA
ShopMartingale.com

Printed in China
20 19 18 17 16 15   8 7 6 5 4 3 2 1

Library of Congress Cataloging-in-Publication Data
is available upon request.

ISBN: 978-1-60468-614-2

DEDICATION

To my husband and children. You give me more love, joy, and hope than I ever knew was possible.

Mission Statement

Dedicated to providing quality products and service to inspire creativity.

Credits

PUBLISHER AND CHIEF VISIONARY OFFICER
Jennifer Erbe Keltner

EDITORIAL DIRECTOR
Karen Costello Soltys

ACQUISITIONS EDITOR
Karen M. Burns

TECHNICAL EDITOR
Nancy Mahoney

COPY EDITOR
Marcy Heffernan

DESIGN DIRECTOR
Paula Schlosser

PHOTOGRAPHER
Brent Kane

PRODUCTION MANAGER
Regina Girard

COVER AND
INTERIOR DESIGNER
Adrienne Smitke

ILLUSTRATOR
Christine Erikson

Contents

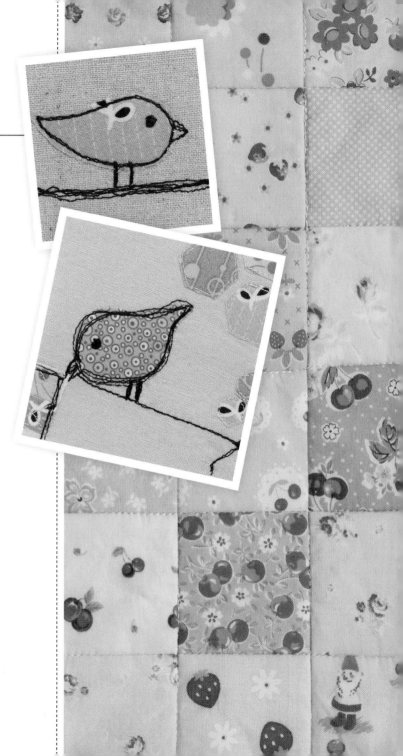

Bonus Pattern Online!
*Visit ShopMartingale.com/Extras
to download "Peekabook-Bird
Churn Dash Table Runner" for free.*

Introduction

I love to sew, and I love quilts! My love for quilting began over a dozen years ago, when I ventured to make my own quilt. I lived in Lancaster County, Pennsylvania, at the time and was surrounded by beautiful Amish quilts. I longed to have one, but unfortunately it just wasn't in my budget. Having always been a do-it-yourself kinda gal, I knew I could make a quilt of my own. With the sewing machine my mother-in-law had given me and very basic sewing skills, I was off and running!

Although I love hand sewing and slowing things down a bit, I must admit that making something from start to finish in just a few hours is very appealing to me. Mini quilts satisfy that desire perfectly. The projects in this book all come from bird quilts I started making about five years ago. They were something I could play around with for an hour or so in the morning, before everyone was awake, and see to completion.

The beauty of these quilts is that they're small enough that I can make them on a whim. And you can too! Just grab some scraps of linen and pretty cotton prints, a bit of fusible web, a pencil, and get started. Until I was asked to create a few online tutorials for the bird quilts, I had never made a template for them. I liked to draw the birds as I worked. Every quilt was just a little different with its own personality. Most of the quilts I make have some sort of meaning or reason behind them, and I enjoy stitching birds for different occasions. I like to use the birds or other appliqué pieces to represent family members, a holiday, or a person. I've even made an Elvis bird.

My hope is that you can take something you learn from this book and make it your own. Quilting is indeed an art filled with exquisitely intricate stitches, perfect piecing, and prizewinning beauties, but there is nothing wrong with letting your hair down, throwing caution to the wind, and just making something that makes you happy no matter your skill level.

Happy sewing!

Erin

Free-Motion Appliqué

The projects in this book are all made using raw-edge appliqué. Most of them also incorporate a fun technique called sketch appliqué or free-motion appliqué. For this technique, you'll need a free-motion foot, which is also called a darning foot. You'll need to lower the feed dogs on your machine or cover them using a throat plate especially designed for that purpose. Starting out, I free-motion appliquéd and quilted using a button foot (not to be mistaken for a buttonhole attachment). I reduced the stitch length to 0 and adjusted the pressure on the foot. I appliquéd and quilted this way for a few years until I upgraded my sewing machine. So, you too can make do with what you have.

A free-motion or darning foot can be open toe or a fully closed round foot.

With free-motion sewing, you're in charge of how your fabric is fed through the machine—which is really fun! You can create all sorts of things with this technique, from free-motion quilting to thread drawing and raw-edge appliqué. It's a fun way to step outside your comfort zone and just play with fabric and thread. The majority of the projects in this book use the following free-motion appliqué technique.

Free-Motion Appliqué Supplies

Black or natural-colored 50-weight thread
Free-motion or darning foot
Latex or quilting gloves (optional)
Lightweight fusible interfacing
Lightweight paper-backed fusible web
Universal needles, size 80/12

Preparing the Appliqués

1. Fuse the fusible side of the interfacing (the bumpy side) to the wrong side of the background fabric. Using a fusible interfacing stabilizes the background fabric and reduces puckering that can be caused by the stitches.

2. Using a pencil or permanent marker, trace each shape the number of times indicated on the pattern onto the paper side of the fusible web. Be sure to leave about ½" between shapes.

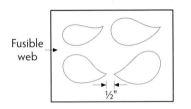

Fusible web

½"

3. Roughly cut out the fusible-web shape, leaving a margin of about ⅛" all around the marked line.

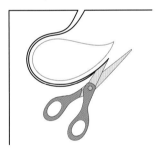

4. Place the shape, fusible-web side down, on the wrong side of the appropriate appliqué fabric. Follow the manufacturer's instructions to fuse the shape to the fabric.

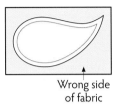

Wrong side of fabric

5. Cut out the fabric shape on the drawn line and remove the paper backing.

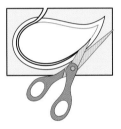

6. Position the appliqué shape, adhesive side down, on the right side of the background fabric and press.

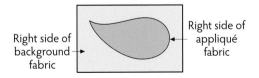

Right side of background fabric

Right side of appliqué fabric

Stitching the Appliqués

1. Thread your machine with a good-quality 50-weight thread in black and use the same thread in the bobbin. Install a new needle; I use a universal 80/12. Swap out your regular presser foot for a free-motion or darning foot. Lower or cover the feed dogs.

Using Gloves

A pair of latex or quilting gloves is very helpful when free-motion sewing. Gloves will give you extra control over the movement of the fabric.

2. Put on latex or quilting gloves, if you use them. Place the appliqué section of your project under the machine needle. Lower the presser foot and, using the hand wheel or the needle up/down button if you have one, sink the needle down into the fabric, and then let it come all the way back up. Gently tug the thread tail until the bobbin thread loops up through the surface of your quilt. Pull on that loop until the bobbin tail is all the way on the surface. Now you're ready to begin.

3. Holding both threads, sew two or three stitches in the same spot to secure the threads. Then begin sewing around the appliqué, stitching about ⅛" from the raw edge of the appliqué piece as shown.

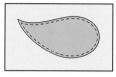

4. Stitch around the appliqué as many times as you would like. I usually stitch around a shape two or three times, which is enough to make it look like a sketch in a notebook. I also make sure I'm not sewing right on top of a previously stitched line. I like some of the stitched lines to go off of the appliqué piece onto the background and some of them to stray from the previously stitched lines a bit, just like a sketch. If you want a more delicate look, stitch around the appliqué just once.

5. Pull both threads to the wrong side of the background; knot and clip the threads.

Sewing Even Stitches

The key to nice, even stitches is to find a balance between how fast you move the fabric and the speed you're sewing. If you move your hands too slowly and your needle is going fast, the stitches will be short and look bunched up. If you move your hands faster than your needle is moving, you'll make long stitches. You want a good balance, somewhere in the middle. I try to use a faster speed and move my fabric at a moderate pace. If you feel you don't have control of the fabric, slow down a bit. The best advice I can give is to practice, practice, practice! Make a few sample pieces with scraps and practice free-motion appliqué until you're comfortable controlling the fabric.

Lovebirds

*T*his little quilt reminds me of being young and in love, exchanging little notes and carving our initials into a tree. It's perfect for using up your favorite scraps. I love the pop of aqua used for one of the birds. Very simple and totally adorable!

FINISHED SIZE: 12½" x 14½"

Materials

Yardage is based on 42"-wide fabric.

½ yard of natural-colored linen for appliqué background

Scraps of 10 assorted red and pink prints for heart and bird appliqués

Scraps of 2 aqua prints for bird and envelope appliqués

¼ yard of fabric for binding

1 fat quarter (18" x 21") of fabric for backing

15" x 18" piece of batting

13½" x 16½" piece of lightweight fusible interfacing

⅛ yard of lightweight fusible web

Black thread for free-motion appliqué

Cutting

From the natural-colored linen, cut:

1 rectangle, 13½" x 15½"

From the binding fabric, cut:

2 strips, 2½" x 42"

Preparing the Appliqués

For detailed instructions, refer to "Free-Motion Appliqué" on page 6. The patterns for the hearts, birds, and envelope are on page 15.

1. Place the interfacing fusible side down on the linen. Press until fused. Set aside.

2. Trace the patterns as follows onto the paper side of the fusible web, leaving at least ½"

between shapes: one each of hearts A and C, two each of hearts D and E, three of heart D, two birds, and one envelope. Cut out the fusible-web shapes, leaving ⅛" of web outside the traced line.

3. Place the fusible side of each shape onto the wrong side of the corresponding fabrics. As instructed on the pattern, place the hearts on red and pink prints, one bird on a red print, and the other bird and envelope on aqua prints. Using an iron, fuse the web to the fabric.

4. Cut out the appliqué pieces on the traced line and remove the paper backing.

5. Find the center of the linen rectangle by gently pressing the piece in half vertically and horizontally.

6. Place the hearts in the upper-left corner of the linen rectangle, about 2" down from the top and 1¼" in from the left edge, to mimic leaves on a tree. Overlap the hearts as shown in the appliqué placement guide at right. Fuse in place.

7. Again referring to the placement guide or photo on page 11 for placement guidance, place the birds on the linen rectangle with the red bird roughly centered on the vertical crease. The birds should face each other, with the aqua bird on the right. Place the envelope between the birds, leaving about ¼" between

the envelope and each bird. This will give you room to stitch their beaks.

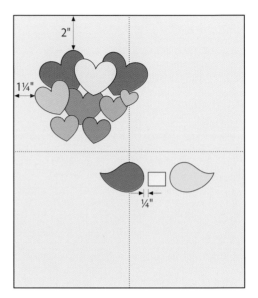

Appliqué placement guide

Stitching the Appliqués

Prepare your machine for free-motion appliqué as described in "Free-Motion Appliqué." Make two or three stitches at the beginning and end of each appliqué step before you lift the presser foot and needle and move to the next appliqué piece.

1. Starting along one side of a smaller, complete heart, sew along the edge of the appliqué piece until you have gone around the heart completely one time. Sew around the heart one more time.

2. Lift the presser foot and needle and move to the next heart. Stitch around the heart two times. Repeat the process until you have stitched along the edge of each heart two times.

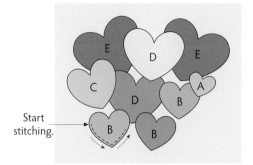

3. Starting along the round side of the red bird, sew along the edge of the appliqué piece until you have gone completely around the bird one time. Sew around the bird one more time.

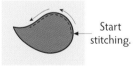

4. Stitch a triangular-shaped beak onto the linen at the spot where you began. Sew over this one more time.

5. Lift the presser foot and needle and move to the area of the bird where the eye should be; sew in a circular motion to make a small eye for the bird.

6. Move to the bottom or belly of the bird and stitch two parallel lines about ⅛" to ¼" apart to make the bird's legs.

7. Repeat steps 3–6 to stitch the aqua bird.

8. Move to the envelope. Referring to the photo above and on page 11, stitch around the envelope two times. Stitch lines to represent the flap and back of the envelope.

9. To stitch the left side of the tree trunk, start about ½" from the base of the hearts and stitch a line down and back, about 6¾" long. To stitch the right side of the trunk, start about ⅜" from the base of the hearts and stitch a line to about where the birds are. Then stitch a branch out toward the birds, making sure their legs fall on the stitch line. Stitch back over the same line to the base of the hearts. To finish the tree, start on the right side at the base of the trunk and stitch up to the branch, stopping about 1" from the branch. Stitch the bottom of the branch; then stitch back to the base of the trunk. On the tree trunk, stitch *U + Me,* and then stitch a heart and arrow.

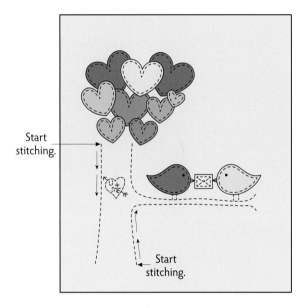

10. Pull all the threads to the back of the linen background; knot and clip the threads.

11. Press well. Trim the appliquéd piece to measure 12½" x 14½", trimming equally on all sides.

Quilting and Finishing

1. Layer the quilt top with batting and backing. Baste the layers together.

2. Quilt as desired. This quilt was quilted with swirls using a thread color that matches the linen background.

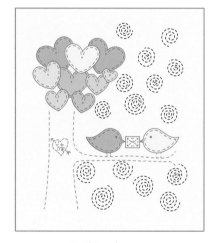

Quilting diagram

3. Trim the excess batting and backing even with the quilt top. Referring to "Binding" on page 77, use the 2½"-wide binding strips to make and attach the binding.

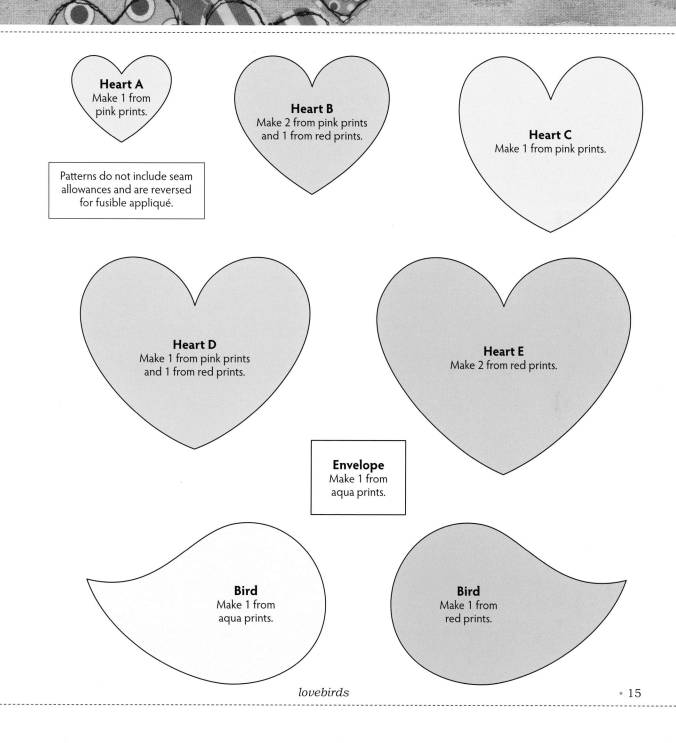

Heart A
Make 1 from pink prints.

Heart B
Make 2 from pink prints and 1 from red prints.

Heart C
Make 1 from pink prints.

Patterns do not include seam allowances and are reversed for fusible appliqué.

Heart D
Make 1 from pink prints and 1 from red prints.

Heart E
Make 2 from red prints.

Envelope
Make 1 from aqua prints.

Bird
Make 1 from aqua prints.

Bird
Make 1 from red prints.

lovebirds

Bird Family

This fun project is similar to one of my first bird quilts. You can make this quilt to represent your own family or a friend's family. Simply appliqué one bird for each family member. Aqua and yellow are a cheerful color combination and give this little quilt a modern vibe.

FINISHED SIZE: 17" x 11"

Materials

Yardage is based on 42"-wide fabric.

¼ yard of natural-colored linen for appliqué background

¼ yard *total* of assorted aqua prints for patchwork border and bird appliqués

¼ yard *total* of assorted yellow prints for patchwork border and bird appliqués

¼ yard of fabric for binding
1 fat quarter (18" x 21") of fabric for backing
14" x 20" piece of batting
6" x 15" piece of lightweight fusible interfacing
4" x 8" piece of lightweight fusible web
Black thread for free-motion appliqué

Cutting

From the natural-colored linen, cut:
1 rectangle, 6" x 15"

From the assorted yellow prints, cut:
25 squares, 2" x 2"

From the assorted aqua prints, cut:
25 squares, 2" x 2"

From the binding fabric, cut:
2 strips, 2½" x 42"

Preparing the Appliqués

For detailed instructions, refer to "Free-Motion Appliqué" on page 6. The patterns for the birds are on page 20.

1. Place the interfacing fusible side down on the linen rectangle. Press until fused. Set aside.

2. Trace the number of birds indicated on the patterns onto the paper side of the fusible web, leaving at least ½" between shapes. Cut out the fusible-web shapes, leaving ⅛" of web outside the traced line.

3. Place the fusible side of each shape onto the wrong side of the corresponding fabric. As instructed on the patterns, place two birds on aqua prints and three birds on yellow prints. Using an iron, fuse the web to the fabric.

4. Cut out the appliqué pieces on the traced lines and remove the paper backing.

5. Find the center of the linen rectangle by gently pressing the piece in half vertically and horizontally.

6. Center the bird appliqués on the linen, spacing them about ½" to ¾" apart and leaving at least 1½" in from each side of the linen. Fuse in place.

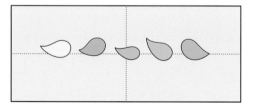

Appliqué placement guide

Stitching the Appliqués

Prepare your machine for free-motion appliqué as described in "Free-Motion Appliqué." Make two or three stitches at the beginning and end of each appliqué step before you lift the presser foot and needle and move to the next appliqué piece.

1. Starting along the round side of the bird, sew along the edge of the appliqué piece until you have gone around the bird completely one time. Sew around the bird one more time.

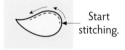

Start stitching.

2. Stitch a triangular-shaped beak onto the linen at the spot where you began. Sew over this one more time.

3. Lift the presser foot and needle and move to the area of the bird where the eye should be; sew in a circular motion to make a small eye for the bird.

4. Move to the bottom or belly of the bird and stitch two parallel lines about ⅛" to ¼" apart to make the bird's legs.

5. Repeat steps 1–4 to stitch around each bird.

6. About 1½" from the left edge of the linen, start stitching the branch that the birds rest on. Stitch toward the right of the linen,

stopping about 1½" from the edge. Go back to the left side and then back to the right side, making sure that your stitching lines touch the birds' legs.

Start stitching.

7. Pull all the threads to the back of the linen background; knot and clip the threads.

8. Press well. Trim the appliquéd piece to measure 14" x 5", trimming equally on all sides.

Adding the Patchwork Border

Replace the free-motion foot with your general sewing presser foot.

1. Arrange the aqua and yellow squares in a pleasing manner around the appliquéd piece as shown in the photo on page 17.

2. Sew three squares together to make a side border. Press the seam allowances in one direction. Repeat to make a second side border.

Make 2.

3. Sew 11 squares together to make a strip. Press the seam allowances toward the right. Make a second strip and press the seam allowances toward the left. Then sew the strips together to make the top border. Press the seam allowances in one direction. Repeat to make the bottom border.

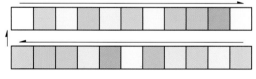

Make 2.

4. Sew the borders from step 2 to the left and right sides of the appliquéd piece. Press the seam allowances toward the borders. Sew the

bird family

borders from step 3 to the top and bottom of the appliquéd piece. Press the seam allowances toward the borders.

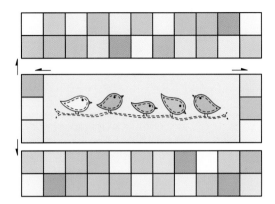

Quilting and Finishing

1. Layer the quilt top with batting and backing. Baste the layers together.

2. Quilt as desired. This quilt was outline quilted ⅛" from the edge of the patchwork. Then two parallel lines were stitched, starting ½" from the first line and spaced ½" apart.

3. Trim the excess batting and backing even with the quilt top. Referring to "Binding" on page 77, use the 2½"-wide binding strips to make and attach the binding.

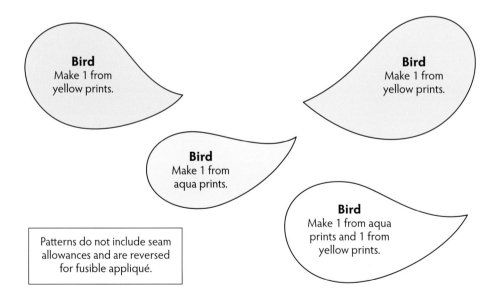

Bird
Make 1 from
yellow prints.

Bird
Make 1 from
yellow prints.

Bird
Make 1 from
aqua prints.

Bird
Make 1 from aqua
prints and 1 from
yellow prints.

Patterns do not include seam
allowances and are reversed
for fusible appliqué.

sweet tweets

Bright and Cheery Bird Pillow

Add a pop of sunshine to any room with this bright and cheery pillow! It's the perfect size for a little one to use during story time. Instructions for adding a matching hand-crocheted edging are provided, but you could substitute a purchased trim.

FINISHED SIZE: 12" x 12"

Materials

Yardage is based on 42"-wide fabric.

⅜ yard of natural-colored linen for appliqué background

⅛ yard *total* of assorted pink prints for patchwork-border and flower-petal appliqués

⅛ yard *total* of assorted yellow florals for patchwork-border and bird appliqués

1 square, at least 4" x 4", of yellow gingham for sun appliqué

½ yard of white solid or natural muslin for pillow-cover-front backing

⅓ yard of pink ticking or stripe for pillow-cover back

9½" x 9½" piece of lightweight fusible interfacing

10" x 10" piece of lightweight fusible web

16" x 16" piece of cotton batting

Black thread for free-motion appliqué

2 skeins of yellow embroidery floss to match fabric

1 skein (approximately 200 yards) of worsted-weight yellow yarn to match floss and fabric for crocheted edging*

Size G crochet hook

Embroidery needle

12" x 12" pillow form

*If you don't crochet, you can substitute 2 yards of lace trim, rickrack, or pom-poms.

Cutting

From the natural-colored linen, cut:

1 square, 9½" x 9½"

From the assorted pink prints, cut:

10 squares, 2½" x 2½"

Continued on page 23

Continued from page 21

From the assorted yellow florals, cut:
10 squares, 2½" x 2½"

From the white solid or muslin, cut:
1 square, 16" x 16"

From the pink ticking or stripe, cut:
2 rectangles, 8½" x 12½"

Preparing the Appliqués

For detailed instructions, refer to "Free-Motion Appliqué" on page 6. The patterns for the bird, sun, and flower petal are on page 27.

1. Place the 9½" square of interfacing fusible side down on the linen square. Press until fused. Set aside.

2. Trace the bird, the sun, and five flower petals onto the paper side of the fusible web, leaving at least ½" between shapes. Cut out the fusible-web shapes, leaving ⅛" of web outside the traced line.

3. Place the fusible side of each shape onto the wrong side of the corresponding fabric. As instructed on the pattern, place the sun on the yellow gingham, the bird on the yellow floral, and the five petals on the pink prints. Using an iron, fuse the web to the fabric.

4. Cut out the appliqué pieces on the traced lines and remove the paper backing.

5. Find the center of the linen 9½" square by gently pressing the piece in half vertically and horizontally.

6. Place the bird appliqué in the lower-left quadrant. Fuse in place.

7. Place the flower petals in the lower-right quadrant. Position them close to the horizontal pressed line, arranging them like a flower. Fuse in place.

8. Place the sun in the upper-left quadrant, aligning the corners of the linen and the appliqué piece. Fuse in place.

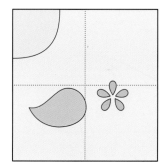

Appliqué placement guide

Stitching the Appliqués

Prepare your machine for free-motion appliqué as described in "Free-Motion Appliqué." Make two or three stitches at the beginning and end of each appliqué step before you lift the presser foot and needle and move to the next appliqué.

1. Starting along the round side of the bird, sew along the edge of the appliqué piece until you have gone around the bird completely one time. Sew around the bird two more times.

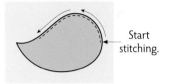

Start stitching.

2. Stitch a triangular-shaped beak onto the linen at the spot where you began. Sew over this two more times.

3. Lift the presser foot and needle and move to the area of the bird where the eye should be; sew in a circular motion to make a small eye for the bird.

4. Move to the bottom or belly of the bird and stitch two parallel lines about ⅛" to ¼" apart to make the bird's legs.

5. Move to the flower petals. Stitch around each petal three times.

6. To make a stem, find the center of the petals and stitch a line downward from the center about 1½" to 1¾" long, stopping at about the same point as the bird's feet, so that the flower stem and bird's feet are in line. Sew back up the stem and down again, stopping at the bottom of the stem. Stitch a leaf onto each side of the stem at the bottom.

7. About 1¾" from the left edge of the linen, below the bird's legs, start stitching the ground that the bird and flower rest on. Stitch toward the right of the linen, stopping about 1¼" from the edge. Go back to the left side and then back to the right side, making sure that your stitching lines touch the bird's legs, flower stem, and leaves.

8. Move to the sun appliqué. Start at the top curved edge of the sun and outline the appliqué. To stitch the squiggly sun rays, start about 1" from the top edge of the linen. Stitch a ray out and back, about 1" long. Continue stitching around the sun, stopping every ¼" to ½" to make a sun ray. Stitch the last sun ray no closer than 1" from the left edge so that you won't lose any of the sun rays during trimming or in the seam allowance. Sew back up to the top of the sun, going over the edge and rays that you just made.

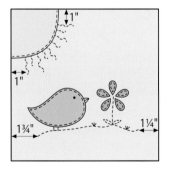

9. Pull all the threads to the back of the linen background; knot and clip the threads. Press

and then trim the appliquéd piece to 8½" x 8½", trimming equally on all sides.

Adding the Patchwork Border

Replace the free-motion foot with your general sewing presser foot.

1. Sew together two yellow and two pink squares to make a patchwork strip for the top border. Repeat to make the bottom border. Sew together three pink and three yellow squares to make a side border. Repeat to make a second side border. Press the seam allowances as indicated.

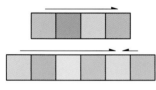

Make 2 of each.

2. Sew the top and bottom borders to the linen square. Make sure the top border has a yellow square on the left and the bottom border has a pink square on the left as shown in the pillow-top assembly diagram at right. Press the seam allowances toward the borders.

3. Sew the side borders to the linen square, with a pink square at the top of the left border and a yellow square at the top of the right border

so that the colors alternate all the way around the pillow top. Press the seam allowances toward the borders.

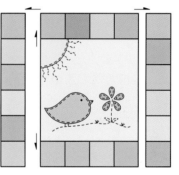

Pillow-top assembly

Quilting

1. Layer the pillow top with batting and the white or muslin 16" square to make a quilt sandwich. Pin baste the layers together.

2. Machine stitch ⅛" from the edge of the patchwork border on each patchwork strip.

3. Trim the pillow top to measure 12½" square.

Assembling the Pillow Cover

1. On each of the pink-ticking rectangles, fold over ¼" on one 12½" edge and press. Fold over ¼" again. Press and stitch along the folded edge.

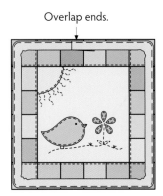

Fold ¼"; press.   Fold again and stitch.

2. If you're planning to crochet trim, skip this step; handmade trim will be added later. If you're using purchased trim, pin it around the entire edge of the border, matching raw edges and overlapping the ends. Baste.

Overlap ends.

Align raw edges, pin, and then baste.

3. Overlap the pillow-cover backs on top of the pillow-cover front, right sides together, as shown. Pin and then stitch using a ¼" seam allowance.

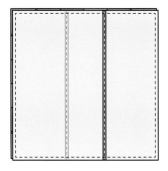

4. Clip the corners, making sure not to clip into the stitching. Turn the pillow cover right side out and gently poke the corners and seams. Press well.

Crocheting the Scalloped Edge

For more details on any of the following steps, go to ShopMartingale.com/HowtoCrochet for free downloadable information.

1. Thread an embroidery needle with all six strands of yellow embroidery floss and blanket-stitch around the entire outside edge

of the pillow. Space the stitches about ½"
apart and ¼" deep. Make 24 stitches on
each side.

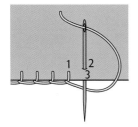

2. Starting at the middle of the pillow's bottom
edge, use the yellow yarn and crochet hook
to slip stitch into the first blanket stitch.
*Double crochet five times into the next
blanket stitch, slip stitch into the next blanket

stitch; repeat from * around, ending with a
slip stitch into the first blanket stitch where
you started.

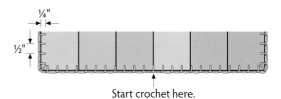

Start crochet here.

3. Pull the yarn through the loop on the hook.
Cut the yarn leaving a 6" tail, and weave it
into the scalloped edge.

4. Insert the pillow form.

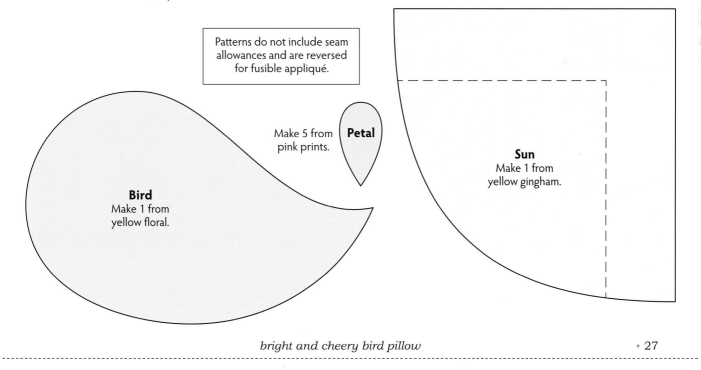

Patterns do not include seam
allowances and are reversed
for fusible appliqué.

Make 5 from **Petal**
pink prints.

Bird
Make 1 from
yellow floral.

Sun
Make 1 from
yellow gingham.

Early Bird Place Mat

B righten up the breakfast table with a cheerful place mat. It's a wonderful way to use up precious scraps you may have saved. I adorned this one with handmade crochet trim, but you could use purchased trim, rickrack, or ribbon.

FINISHED SIZE: 16½" x 12½"

Materials

Yardage is based on 42"-wide fabric.

¼ yard of natural-colored linen for appliqué background

¼ yard *total* of assorted aqua, pink, green, and yellow prints for patchwork

Scrap, at least 3" x 4", of aqua polka dot for bird appliqué

¼ yard of pink print for binding

1 fat quarter (18" x 21") of fabric for backing

15" x 19" piece of batting

7½" x 13½" piece of lightweight fusible interfacing

3" x 4" piece of lightweight fusible web

Black thread for free-motion appliqué

2 skeins of aqua-colored embroidery floss to match fabric for crocheted edging*

Size E crochet hook

*If you don't crochet, you can substitute ½ yard of lace trim or rickrack.

Cutting

From the natural-colored linen, cut:
1 rectangle, 7½" x 13½"

From the assorted aqua, pink, green, and yellow prints, cut a *total* of:
30 squares, 2½" x 2½"

From the pink print, cut:
2 strips, 2½" x 42"

4. Cut out the appliqué piece on the traced lines and remove the paper backing.

5. Find the center of the linen rectangle by gently pressing the piece in half vertically and horizontally.

6. Place the bird in the center of the linen, slightly above the crease line. Fuse in place.

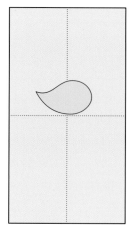

Appliqué placement guide

Preparing the Appliqué

For detailed instructions, refer to "Free-Motion Appliqué" on page 6.

1. Place the interfacing fusible side down on the linen rectangle. Press until fused. Set aside.

2. Using the bird pattern on page 33, trace the bird onto the paper side of the fusible web. Cut out the fusible-web shape, leaving ⅛" of web outside the traced line.

3. Place the fusible side of the shape onto the wrong side of the aqua polka dot. Using an iron, fuse the web to the fabric.

Stitching the Appliqué

Prepare your machine for free-motion appliqué as described in "Free-Motion Appliqué." Make two or three stitches at the beginning and end of each appliqué step before you lift the presser foot and needle and move to the next appliqué piece.

1. Starting along the round side of the bird, sew along the edge of the appliqué piece until you have gone around the bird completely one time. Sew around the bird one more time.

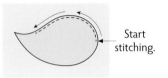

Start stitching.

2. Stitch a triangular-shaped beak onto the linen at the spot where you began. Sew over this two more times.

3. Lift the presser foot and needle and move to the area of the bird where the eye should be; sew in a circular motion to make a small eye for the bird.

4. Move to the bottom or belly of the bird and stitch two parallel lines about ⅛" to ¼" apart to make the bird's legs.

5. To make the tree trunk, start on the left edge about 2½" down from the top and stitch a line downward, stopping about 2" from the bottom edge. Sew up the trunk and back down again. Continue stitching lines until the trunk is about 1¼" wide.

6. When the tree trunk is the desired width, start stitching a branch for the bird to rest on. Stitch to the right of the linen, along the horizontal crease, stopping about 1½" from the edge. Go back to the right, stitch up the

trunk, down the trunk, and then back to the right, making sure the stitching lines touch the bird's legs. Stitch back and forth to the desired thickness.

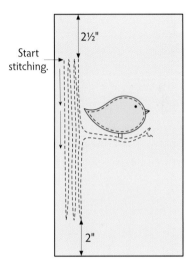

2½"

Start stitching.

2"

7. Pull all the threads to the back of the linen background; knot and clip the threads.

8. Press well. Trim the appliquéd piece to measure 6½" x 12½", trimming equally on all sides.

Making the Patchwork Piece

Replace the free-motion foot with your general sewing presser foot.

1. Lay out the aqua, pink, green, and yellow squares in six rows of five squares each. When you are pleased with the arrangement,

sew the squares together in rows. Press the seam allowances in opposite directions from row to row.

2. Sew the rows together. Press the seam allowances in one direction. The patchwork piece should measure 10½" x 12½".

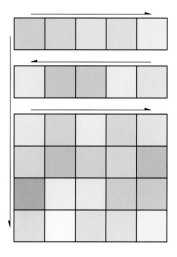

Making the Crocheted Trim

For more details on any of the following steps, go to ShopMartingale.com/HowtoCrochet for free downloadable information.

1. Use the aqua embroidery floss and crochet hook to make a 13"-long foundation chain, turn the work, and single crochet into each chain stitch to the end.

2. Turn the work, and single crochet into the next two stitches, *double crochet five stitches into the next stitch, skip one stitch, slip stitch into the next stitch; repeat from * across, ending with a slip stitch.

3. Pull the yarn through the loop on the hook. Cut the yarn, leaving a 6" tail.

Assembling the Place Mat

1. Place the crocheted trim along the right edge of the linen with the scallops facing toward the bird and the edge of the trim even with the linen. Pin in place.

2. Layer the patchwork piece on top of the linen and crocheted trim, right sides together. Sew the pieces together. Press the seam allowances toward the patchwork piece so that the scallops lie flat on the linen.

3. Topstitch ⅛" from the edge of the patchwork.

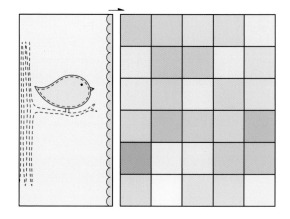

Quilting and Finishing

1. Layer the quilt top with batting and backing. Baste the layers together.

2. Quilt as desired. The patchwork piece on this place mat was quilted in the ditch.

3. Trim the excess batting and backing even with the quilt top. Referring to "Binding" on page 77, use the pink 2½"-wide strips to make and attach the binding.

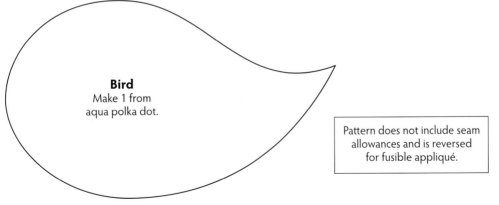

Bird
Make 1 from
aqua polka dot.

Pattern does not include seam
allowances and is reversed
for fusible appliqué.

Three Little Birds

This is such a happy quilt, it makes my heart sing. Can't you just see these tiny little birds sitting on a branch enjoying a colorful summer day? If you've never made hexagons using paper templates before, this is the perfect opportunity to try them.

FINISHED SIZE: 11" x 17"

Materials

Yardage is based on 42"-wide fabric.

⅜ yard of natural-colored linen for appliqué background

¼ yard *total* of assorted blue and red prints for patchwork border and bird appliqués

¼ yard *total* of assorted green prints for patchwork border and hexagons

⅛ yard *total* of yellow prints for patchwork border

¼ yard of green stripe for binding

1 fat quarter (18" x 21") of fabric for backing

13" x 19" piece of batting

10" x 16" piece of lightweight fusible interfacing

2" x 4" piece of lightweight fusible web

Black thread for free-motion appliqué

Paper for hexagon templates

Cutting

From the natural-colored linen, cut:

1 rectangle, 10" x 16"

From the assorted blue, red, green, and yellow prints, cut a *total* of:

32 squares, 2" x 2"

From the remaining assorted green prints, cut:

29 squares, 1½" x 1½"

From the green stripe, cut:

2 strips, 2½" x 42"

Preparing the Hexagons

1. Using the hexagon pattern on page 39, trace 29 hexagons onto paper. Cut out the paper hexagons on the traced lines.

3. With the paper side up, fold the seam allowance over the paper and hand baste the seam allowance in place. Make 29.

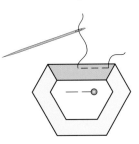

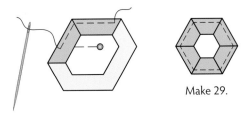

Make 29.

Preparing the Appliqués

For detailed instructions, refer to "Free-Motion Appliqué" on page 6. The patterns for the birds are on page 39.

1. Place the interfacing fusible side down on the linen rectangle. Press until fused. Set aside.

2. Trace one of each bird onto the paper side of the fusible web, leaving at least ½" between shapes. Cut out the fusible-web shapes, leaving ⅛" of web outside the traced line.

2. Center and pin a paper hexagon to the wrong side of each green 1½" square. With the paper side up, trim the excess fabric around each hexagon, leaving a generous ¼" seam allowance all around.

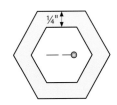

sweet tweets

3. Place the fusible side of each shape on the wrong side of the corresponding fabric. As instructed on the pattern, place two birds on blue prints and one bird on a red print. Using an iron, fuse the web to the fabric.

4. Cut out the appliqué pieces on the traced lines and remove the paper backing.

5. Find the center of the linen rectangle by gently pressing the piece in half vertically and horizontally.

6. Place the birds on the linen, with the left bird on the horizontal centerline and the right bird about ½" below the horizontal centerline and on the left side of the vertical centerline. Fuse in place.

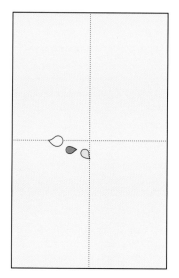

Appliqué placement guide

Stitching the Hexagons

1. Refer to the photo on page 35 for placement guidance. Arrange the hexagons in the upper half of the linen background, leaving about ¼" between the hexagons and about 1½" from the top and right edges.

2. Topstitch around each hexagon. I left the papers in the hexagons for added dimension. If you want to remove the paper, starch the hexagons and press them well. Then make a small slit in the linen and gently remove the paper.

Stitching the Appliqués

Prepare your machine for free-motion appliqué as described in "Free-Motion Appliqué." Make two or three stitches at the beginning and end of each appliqué step before you lift the presser foot and needle and move to the next appliqué piece.

1. Starting along the round side of the bird, sew along the edge of the appliqué piece until you have gone around the bird completely one time. Sew around the bird one more time.

Start stitching.

three little birds

to the right and then back to the left, making sure the stitching lines touch the birds' legs. Stitch back and forth to the desired thickness.

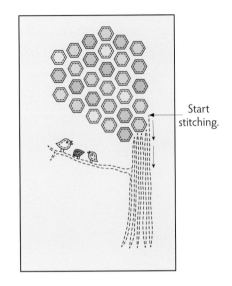

Start stitching.

2. Stitch a triangular-shaped beak onto the linen at the spot where you began. Sew over this two more times.

3. Lift the presser foot and needle and move to the area of the bird where the eye should be; sew in a circular motion to make a small eye for the bird.

4. Move to the bottom or belly of the bird and stitch two parallel lines about ⅛" to ¼" apart to make the bird's legs.

5. Repeat steps 1–4 to stitch around each bird.

6. To make the tree trunk, start under the hexagon about 1½" from the right edge of the linen, and stitch a line downward, stopping about 1½" from the bottom edge. Sew up the trunk and back down again. Continue stitching up and down until the tree trunk is about 1½" wide at the top and 2" wide at the bottom.

7. When the tree trunk is the desired width, start stitching a branch for the birds to rest on. Stitch toward the left of the linen, stopping about 1½" from the edge. Go back

8. Pull all the threads to the back of the linen background; knot and clip the threads. Press and then trim the appliquéd piece to measure 8" x 14", trimming equally on all sides.

Adding the Patchwork Border

Replace the free-motion foot with your general sewing presser foot.

1. Arrange the blue, red, green, and yellow squares in a pleasing manner around the appliquéd piece as shown in the photo on page 35.

sweet tweets

2. Sew five squares together to make the top border. Press the seam allowances in one direction. Repeat to make the bottom border. Sew the borders to the top and bottom of the appliquéd piece. Press the seam allowances toward the borders.

3. Sew 11 squares together to make a side border. Press the seam allowances in the directions indicated. Repeat to make a second side border. Sew these borders to the left and right sides of the appliquéd piece. Press the seam allowances toward the borders.

Quilting and Finishing

1. Layer the quilt top with batting and backing. Baste the layers together.

2. Quilt as desired. This quilt was outline quilted ⅛" from the edge of the patchwork. Then two parallel lines were stitched, starting ½" from the first line and spaced ½" apart.

3. Trim the excess batting and backing even with the quilt top. Referring to "Binding" on page 77, use the green-striped 2½"-wide strips to make and attach the binding.

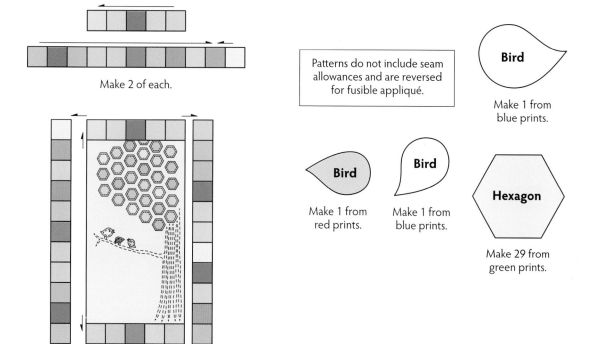

Make 2 of each.

Patterns do not include seam allowances and are reversed for fusible appliqué.

Bird
Make 1 from blue prints.

Bird
Make 1 from red prints.

Bird
Make 1 from blue prints.

Hexagon
Make 29 from green prints.

Birds and Bees Hot Pad

Here's another opportunity to use popular hexagons. This hot pad is a play on the traditional Honey Bee block. I turned the corner appliqués into birds and added a hexagon center instead of the traditional Nine Patch. A bit of crochet edging gives the look of a vintage finishing touch.

FINISHED SIZE: 9" x 9"

Materials

Yardage is based on 42"-wide fabric.

⅛ yard of multicolored floral for bee appliqués

⅛ yard of teal solid for bird appliqués

⅛ yard *total* of assorted teal, chartreuse, green, and pink prints for hexagons

¼ yard of cream solid for background

⅛ yard of cream stripe for background

9" x 9" piece of fabric for backing

9" x 9" piece of Insul-Bright batting

¼ yard of lightweight fusible web

Black and natural-colored thread for free-motion appliqué

2 skeins of fuchsia embroidery floss for crocheted edging*

Size E crochet hook

Embroidery needle

Cardstock for hexagon templates

Spray starch

*If you don't crochet, you can substitute 1 yard of lace trim, rickrack, or pom-poms.

Cutting

From the assorted teal, chartreuse, green, and pink prints, cut a *total* of:

10 squares, 2¾" x 2¾"

From the cream solid, cut:

1 square, 5" x 5"

4 rectangles, 2¾" x 5"

From the cream stripe, cut:

4 squares, 2¾" x 2¾"

Preparing the Hexagons

1. Using the hexagon pattern on page 46, trace 10 hexagons onto cardstock. Cut out the paper hexagons on the traced line.

2. Center and pin a paper hexagon to the wrong side of each print 2¾" square. With the paper side up, trim the excess fabric around each hexagon, leaving a generous ¼" seam allowance all around.

3. With the paper side up, fold the seam allowance over the paper and hand baste the seam allowance in place. Make 10.

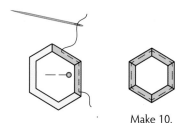

Make 10.

4. Holding two pieces with right sides together and edges even, whipstitch along the fold, using small stitches and taking care not to stitch through the paper. Make two strips with three hexagons and one strip with four hexagons.

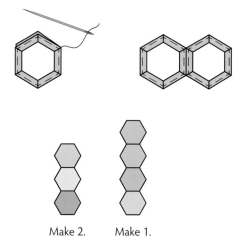

Make 2.   Make 1.

5. In the same way, sew the strips together as shown. Spray with starch and press until dry. Remove the basting stitches and papers. Press again, making sure all of the outer seam allowances are neatly folded under.

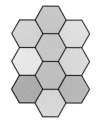

6. Center the hexagon piece on the cream-solid 5" square. The hexagons will extend beyond the square along the top and bottom edges. Topstitch along the side edges of the hexagon piece using natural-colored thread. Trim the hexagon piece to measure 5" x 5".

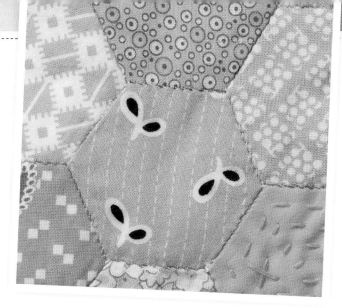

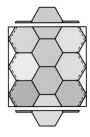

Topstitch and trim.

Assembling the Honey Bee Block

Lay out the cream-striped 2¾" squares, cream-solid rectangles, and hexagon square in three rows. Join the pieces into rows. Press the seam allowances in the directions indicated. Sew the rows together and press away from the center.

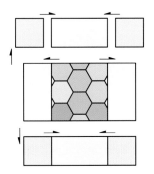

Preparing the Appliqués

For detailed instructions, refer to "Free-Motion Appliqué" on page 6. The pattern for the birds and bees is on page 46.

1. Trace 12 birds/bees onto the paper side of the fusible web, leaving at least ½" between shapes. Cut out the fusible-web shapes, leaving ⅛" of web outside the traced line.

2. Place the fusible side of each shape onto the wrong side of the corresponding fabric. As instructed on the pattern, place four birds on the teal solid and eight bees on the multicolored floral. Using an iron, fuse the web to the fabric.

Stitching the Appliqués

Prepare your machine for free-motion appliqué as described in "Free-Motion Appliqué." Make two or three stitches at the beginning and end of each appliqué step before you lift the presser foot and needle and move to the next appliqué piece.

1. Using black thread and starting along the round side of the bird, sew along the edge of the appliqué piece until you have gone around the bird completely one time. Sew around the bird one more time.

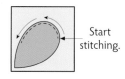

Start stitching.

2. Stitch a triangular-shaped beak onto the linen at the spot where you began. Sew over this one more time.

3. Lift the presser foot and needle and move to the area of the bird where the eye should be; sew in a circular motion to make a small eye for the bird.

4. Move to the bottom or belly of the bird and stitch two parallel lines about ⅛" to ¼" apart to make the bird's legs.

5. Repeat steps 1–4 to stitch around each bird.

6. Move to the bee appliqués. Using natural-colored thread, stitch around each bee.

3. Cut out the appliqué pieces on the traced lines and remove the paper backing.

4. Place a teal bird piece in each corner of the Honey Bee block; the tail should be pointing toward the center and about ⅛" from the seam. Place two multicolored bees on each side of the bird piece with the pointed ends toward the bird and about ⅛" from the seam. Fuse the appliqué pieces in place.

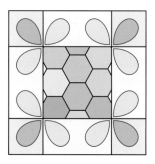

Appliqué placement guide

7. If desired, use six strands of embroidery floss and a backstitch to add embroidery stitches to the hexagons.

8. Pull all the threads to the back of the linen background; knot and clip the threads. Press well.

Finishing the Hot Pad

1. If you're planning to crochet your own trim, skip this step; handmade trim will be added later. If you're using purchased trim, pin it around the entire edge of the appliquéd block, matching the edges and overlapping the ends, and then baste. Add a 4" loop in the upper-left corner with the loop facing in and the raw edges aligned.

2. Place the Insul-Bright on a flat surface. Place the appliquéd block on top of the Insul-Bright, right side up. Then place the backing on top of the appliquéd block, *wrong* side up.

3. Sew all around the hot pad using a ¼" seam allowance. Leave a 4" opening on one side for turning. Clip the corners, making sure not to clip into the stitches.

4. Turn the hot pad right side out. Carefully push out the corners and pull out the trim or rickrack (if applicable). Press well.

5. To close the opening, topstitch ⅛" from the edge all around the hot pad. Then quilt in the ditch along the seamlines.

Crocheting a Scalloped Edge

For more details on any of the following steps, go to ShopMartingale.com/HowtoCrochet for free downloadable information.

1. Thread an embroidery needle with all six strands of embroidery floss and blanket-stitch around the entire outside edge of the hot pad. Space the stitches about ⅜" apart and ¼" deep. Make 23 to 24 stitches on each side.

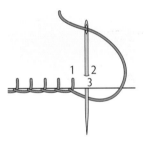

2. Starting at the center of one side of the hot pad, use the fuchsia embroidery floss and crochet hook to slip stitch into the first blanket stitch. *Double crochet five stitches into the next blanket stitch, slip stitch into the next stitch; repeat from * until you reach the corner where you want the hanging loop. Make a chain to the desired length (about 20 chain stitches) and slip stitch into the corner stitch. Slip stitch into the next stitch; then continue the previous pattern of double crochet five into the next blanket stitch, slip stitch into the next blanket stitch, ending with a slip stitch into the first blanket stitch where you started.

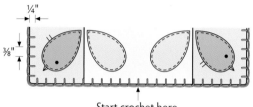

Start crochet here.

3. Pull the floss through the loop on the hook. Cut the floss, leaving a 6" tail, and weave it into the scalloped edge.

Patterns do not include seam allowances.

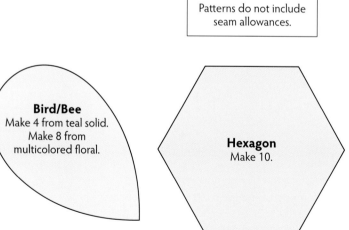

Bird/Bee
Make 4 from teal solid.
Make 8 from multicolored floral.

Hexagon
Make 10.

Rainy Day Bird Coaster

Cuteness meets functionality in this coaster! When you can make a project both cute and functional, you have a great combination. This project is a perfect accompaniment to your morning cuppa, afternoon tea, or nightcap.

FINISHED SIZE: 5" x 5"

Materials

Yardage is based on 42"-wide fabric.

¼ yard of natural-colored linen for appliqué background

⅛ yard *total* of assorted prints for patchwork border, bird, and umbrella appliqués

5½" x 5½" piece of batting

4½" x 5½" piece of lightweight fusible interfacing

3" x 6" piece of lightweight fusible web

Black thread for free-motion appliqué

2 skeins of red embroidery floss for crocheted edging*

1 skein of natural-colored embroidery floss

Size E crochet hook

Embroidery needle

*If you don't crochet, you can substitute 1 yard of lace trim, rickrack, or pom-poms.

Cutting

From the natural-colored linen, cut:

1 rectangle, 4½" x 5½"

1 square, 5½" x 5½"

From the assorted prints, cut:

5 squares, 1½" x 1½"

Preparing the Appliqués

For detailed instructions, refer to "Free-Motion Appliqué" on page 6. The patterns for the bird and umbrella are on page 51.

1. Place the interfacing rectangle fusible side down on the linen rectangle. Press to fuse. Set aside.

2. Trace the bird and umbrella patterns onto the paper side of the fusible web, leaving at least ½" between shapes. Cut out the shapes, leaving ⅛" of web outside the traced line.

3. Place the fusible side of each shape onto the wrong side of an assorted print. Using an iron, fuse the web to the fabric.

4. Cut out the appliqué pieces on the traced lines and remove the paper backing.

5. Gently press the linen rectangle in half vertically and horizontally to find the center. Center the bird on the linen rectangle about ⅞" from the bottom edge. Fuse in place.

6. Place the umbrella about ½" above the bird. Fuse in place.

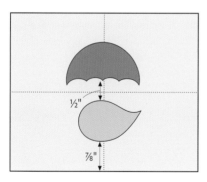

Appliqué placement guide

Stitching the Appliqués

Prepare your machine for free-motion appliqué as described in "Free-Motion Appliqué." Make two or three stitches at the beginning and end of each appliqué step before you lift the presser foot and needle and move to the next appliqué.

1. Starting along the round side of the bird, sew along the edge of the appliqué piece until you have gone completely around the bird twice.

Start stitching.

2. Stitch a triangular-shaped beak onto the linen at the spot where you began. Sew over the beak one more time.

3. Lift the presser foot and needle and move to the area of the bird where the eye should be; sew in a circular motion to make a small eye.

4. Move to the bottom of the bird and stitch two parallel lines ⅛" to ¼" apart for legs.

5. Move to the umbrella. Starting along the top of the curved edge, stitch around the shape three times. From the starting point, stitch a slightly curved line down to the left point on the bottom of the umbrella. Sew back to the top of the umbrella. Then stitch down to the right point and back. Stitch down to the center point. Stitch a line for the umbrella

open. Sew the strip to the top of the linen piece. Press the seam allowances open.

2. Place the coaster top on top of the piece of batting. Topstitch ⅛" from both sides of the patchwork seam.

3. Hand quilt big stitches as shown using an embroidery needle and two strands of natural-colored floss. Press well.

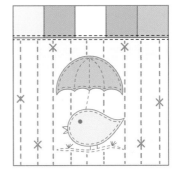

Quilting diagram

handle, stopping at the top of the bird. Stitch back to the top of the umbrella.

6. Stitch the ground that the bird is resting on, starting about 1¾" from the left edge and ¾" from the bottom edge. Stitch toward the right of the linen rectangle, stopping about 1¾" from the right edge. Stitch back to the left side, and then back to the right again, making sure that your stitching lines touch the bird's legs. Stitch a few sprigs of grass.

Assembling the Coaster Top

Replace the free-motion foot with your general sewing presser foot.

1. Sew the five assorted-print squares together to make a strip. Press the seam allowances

Finishing the Coaster

If you're planning to crochet your own trim, skip step 1; handmade trim will be added later.

1. Pin purchased trim around the entire edge of the appliquéd block, matching the edges and overlapping the ends, and then baste.

2. Place the coaster front and the linen 5½" square right sides together. Sew around the coaster using a ¼" seam allowance, leaving a 2" opening on one side for turning. Clip the corners; do not clip into the stitches.

3. Turn the coaster right side out. Carefully push out the corners and pull out the trim. Press well.

4. Fold under the turning gap seam allowances and whipstitch the opening closed. Press well.

Crocheting the Edge

For more details on any of the following steps, go to ShopMartingale.com/HowtoCrochet for free downloadable information.

1. Thread an embroidery needle with all six strands of red embroidery floss. Blanket-stitch around the outside edge of the coaster, spacing stitches about ⅜" apart and ¼" deep. Make 13 to 14 stitches on each side.

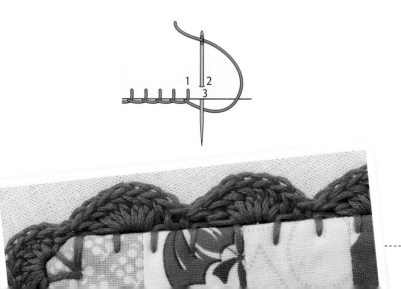

2. Starting at the center of the bottom edge, use the red embroidery floss and crochet hook to slip stitch into the first blanket stitch. *Double crochet seven stitches into the next blanket stitch, slip stitch into the next blanket stitch; repeat from * around, ending with a slip stitch into the first blanket stitch where you started. Pull the floss through the loop on the hook. Cut the floss, leaving a 6" tail, and weave it into the scalloped edge.

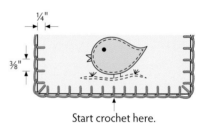

Start crochet here.

Patterns do not include seam allowances and are reversed for fusible appliqué.

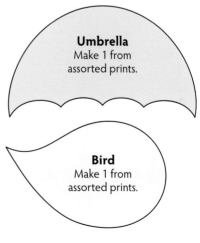

Umbrella
Make 1 from assorted prints.

Bird
Make 1 from assorted prints.

Birds Holding a Quilt

> **W**hat could be cuter than two little birds sitting on a wash line holding a quilt? Use this pint-sized project to add a splash of color in your sewing room or to brighten a friend's day.

FINISHED SIZE: 14½" x 12½"

Materials

Yardage is based on 42"-wide fabric.

⅜ yard of natural-colored linen for appliqué background

¼ yard *total* of assorted pink, blue, yellow, red, and gray prints for patchwork border

¼ yard of assorted green prints for patchwork border and hexagons

¼ yard of yellow check for binding

1 fat quarter (18" x 21") of fabric for backing

10" x 12" piece of lightweight fusible interfacing

¼ yard of lightweight fusible web

15" x 17" piece of batting

Natural-colored and black thread for free-motion appliqué

Appliqué pressing sheet or parchment paper

Cutting

From the natural-colored linen, cut:
1 rectangle, 10" x 12"

From the assorted pink, blue, yellow, red, gray, and green prints, cut a *total* of:
22 squares, 2½" x 2½"
30 squares, ½" x ½"

From the yellow check, cut:
2 strips, 2½" x 42"

Preparing the Appliqués

For detailed instructions, refer to "Free-Motion Appliqué" on page 6. The patterns for the birds and hexagons are on page 57.

1. Place the interfacing fusible side down on the linen. Press until fused. Set aside.

2. Trace one of each bird, 14 large hexagons, and six small hexagons onto the paper side of the fusible web, leaving at least ½" between shapes. Cut out the fusible-web shapes, leaving ⅛" of web outside the traced line. Set aside a 2½" x 3" rectangle of fusible web for the little quilt.

3. Place the fusible side of each shape on the wrong side of the corresponding fabric. As instructed on the pattern, place each bird on a pink print and the large and small hexagons on the assorted green prints. Using an iron, fuse the web to the fabric.

4. Cut out the appliqué pieces on the traced lines. Cut two of the large hexagons in half as shown in the appliqué placement guide on page 55. Remove the paper backing.

Making the Little Quilt Appliqué

1. Arrange the assorted-print ½" squares in six rows of five squares each on the fusible side of the 2½" x 3" rectangle of fusible web. Place an appliqué pressing sheet or a piece of parchment paper over the squares to protect your iron. Carefully iron on top of the little squares to fuse them in place. *Do not* remove the paper backing yet.

2. Using natural-colored thread, topstitch the little quilt diagonally in both directions

through each square to look like crosshatch quilting.

3. Gently peel off the paper backing from the appliqué piece.

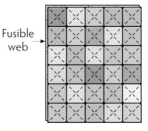

Fusible web →

Topstitch.

Arranging the Appliqués

Refer to the photo on page 53 and the appliqué placement guide on page 55 for placement guidance as needed.

1. Find the center of the linen rectangle by gently pressing the piece in half vertically and horizontally.

2. Place the birds about 2½" apart and ½" above the horizontal pressed line with their bodies pointed slightly downward. Fuse in place.

3. Place the little quilt between the two birds just above the horizontal pressed line, leaving about ¼" on each side between the birds and the little quilt so that you have room to stitch the birds' beaks. The beaks will touch the quilt as if holding it. Fuse in place.

4. Place three small hexagons about ½" above the horizontal pressed line and about 1" to 1¼" from the end of each bird. Fuse in place.

5. Place seven large hexagons about ¼" apart and about ⅜" to ½" above the small hexagons and bird on each side. Fuse in place.

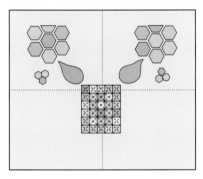

Appliqué placement guide

Stitching the Appliqués

Prepare your machine for free-motion appliqué as described in "Free-Motion Appliqué." Make two or three stitches at the beginning and end of each appliqué step before you lift the presser foot and needle and move to the next appliqué piece.

1. Stitch around each hexagon using natural-colored thread.

2. To make a tree trunk, use black thread to stitch a line downward, starting below the large hexagons on the left side and stopping 1½" from the bottom edge of the linen. Sew up the trunk and back down, and then up the trunk again and back down, stopping at the top of the small hexagons. Starting below the small hexagons, stitch a line downward and back up three times to complete the trunk. Repeat the process to make the tree trunk on the right side of the linen.

3. Starting along the round side of the bird on the left, begin sewing along the edge of the appliqué piece until you have gone around the bird completely one time. Sew around the bird one more time.

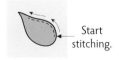

Start stitching.

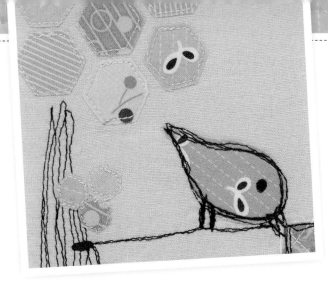

4. Stitch a triangular-shaped beak onto the linen at the spot where you began. Sew over this two more times.

5. Lift the presser foot and needle and move to the area of the bird where the eye should be; sew in a circular motion to make a small eye for the bird.

6. Move to the bottom or belly of the bird and stitch two parallel lines about ⅛" to ¼" apart to make the bird's legs.

7. Repeat steps 3–6 to stitch around the bird on the right.

8. Move to the little quilt. Stitch around the little quilt three times.

9. On the left tree trunk, stitch toward the right of the linen along the horizontal pressed line, making sure that the birds' legs touch the line and the quilt hangs from the stitched line. Stitch back to the left and stitch a loop and string on the left tree trunk so that the clothesline looks like it's tied to the tree trunk. Repeat to stitch a line, loop, and string on the right tree trunk.

10. Pull all the threads to the back of the linen background; knot and clip the threads. Press, and then trim the appliquéd piece to measure 10½" x 8½", trimming equally on all sides.

Adding the Patchwork Border

Replace the free-motion foot with your general sewing presser foot.

1. Arrange the pink, blue, yellow, red, gray, and green 2½" squares in a pleasing manner around the appliquéd piece as shown in the photo on page 53.

2. Sew five squares together to make the top border. Press the seam allowances in one direction. Repeat to make the bottom border. Sew the borders to the top and bottom of the appliquéd piece. Press the seam allowances toward the borders.

3. Sew six squares together to make a side border. Press the seam allowances in the directions indicated. Repeat to make a second side border.

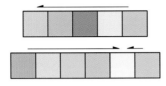

Make 2 of each.

4. Sew these borders to the left and right sides of the appliquéd piece. Press the seam allowances toward the borders.

Quilting and Finishing

1. Layer the quilt top with batting and backing. Baste the layers together.

2. Quilt as desired. This quilt was outline quilted ⅛" from the edge of the patchwork. Then three parallel lines were stitched, starting ½" from the first line and spaced ½" apart.

3. Trim the excess batting and backing even with the quilt top. Referring to "Binding" on page 77, use the yellow-check 2½"-wide strips to make and attach the binding.

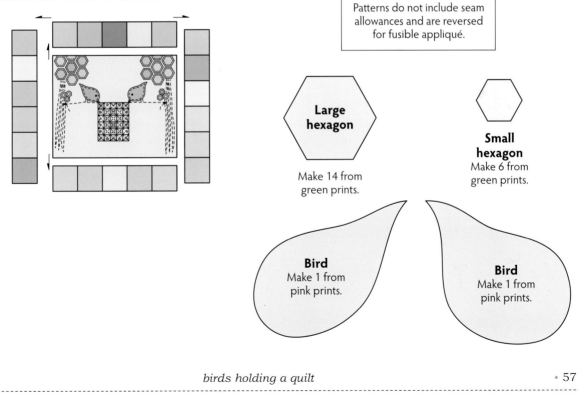

Patterns do not include seam allowances and are reversed for fusible appliqué.

Large hexagon
Make 14 from green prints.

Small hexagon
Make 6 from green prints.

Bird
Make 1 from pink prints.

Bird
Make 1 from pink prints.

Strawberry Fields Bird

I love strawberries as much as birds do, so I had to stitch them into a quilt. With its Courthouse Steps blocks and soft, delicate colors, this quilt has more of a traditional feel. For a cohesive look, choose a pack of charm squares to make the blocks.

FINISHED SIZE: 20" x 24½"
FINISHED BLOCK: 4½" x 4½"

Materials

Yardage is based on 42"-wide fabric.

½ yard *total* of 16 assorted tan or light background prints for blocks and flower appliqués

⅜ yard of white or cream solid for border

¼ yard *total* of 4 red prints for blocks and strawberry appliqués

¼ yard *total* of 3 green prints for blocks, strawberry tops, and flower-leaf appliqués

⅛ yard *total* of 4 aqua prints for blocks

⅛ yard *total* of 2 pink prints for blocks

⅛ yard *total* of 2 yellow prints for blocks

⅛ yard of red solid for blocks

⅛ yard of tan print for blocks

Scrap, at least 3" x 4½", of aqua solid for bird appliqué

⅓ yard of red floral for binding

¾ yard of fabric for backing

23" x 27" piece of batting

Light-colored thread for free-motion appliqué

1 skein of green embroidery floss for vines

1 skein of aqua embroidery floss for bird

1 skein of brown embroidery floss for bird's beak, eye, and legs

Embroidery needle

Removable marking pen

Before You Begin

This quilt is made of 12 blocks, each with a red-solid center square surrounded by logs of four different prints. When the blocks are set together, the print on each side of the block matches the print on the adjacent block, so careful planning up front is essential. To make the layout easier to plan, cutting

is organized by light prints and colored prints. You'll be cutting enough pieces from each print to use in two blocks. (Some prints will only be used once; cut this way, you'll have the option of using each color where you'd like.) Once the pieces are cut, use the illustration on page 61 to plan your color placement so that you can make sure your finished Courthouse Steps blocks form the Chinese lantern effect when sewn together.

Cutting

From the red solid, cut:
12 squares, 1" x 1"

From *each of 8* assorted light prints, cut:
2 rectangles, 1" x 2" (16 total)
2 rectangles, 1" x 3" (16 total)
2 rectangles, 1" x 4" (16 total)
2 squares, 1" x 1" (16 total)

From *each of 8* assorted light prints, cut:
1 rectangle, 1" x 2" (8 total)
1 rectangle, 1" x 3" (8 total)
1 rectangle, 1" x 4" (8 total)
1 square, 1" x 1" (8 total)

From *each* of the green, aqua, pink, yellow, and tan prints, and 3 of the red prints, cut:*
2 rectangles, 1" x 2" (30 total, 6 will be extra)
2 rectangles, 1" x 3" (30 total, 6 will be extra)
2 rectangles, 1" x 4" (30 total, 6 will be extra)
2 rectangles, 1" x 5" (30 total, 6 will be extra)

*The fourth red print will be used for appliqué only.

From the white or cream solid, cut:
2 strips, 3½" x 18½"
2 strips, 3½" x 20"

From the red floral, cut:
3 strips, 2½" x 42"

Assembling the Blocks

Each block is constructed using two light prints, two colored prints, and one red-solid square. The colored rectangles always run horizontally in the blocks. The light rectangles always run vertically in the blocks. Press the seam allowances as you go toward the newly added piece.

1. Sew two different light-print 1" squares to opposite sides of a red-solid square. Then add two different colored 1" x 2" rectangles to the top and bottom of the center unit as shown.

2. Sewing matching colors together as you go, sew light-print 1" x 2" rectangles to the left and right sides of the unit from step 1. Then add colored-print 1" x 3" rectangles to the top and bottom of the center unit as shown.

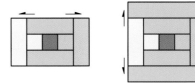

3. Continue adding light and colored rectangles, ending with colored 1" x 5" rectangles. Repeat the process to make a total of 12 blocks.

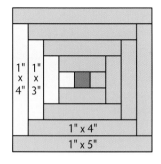

Fabric Placement

Be mindful of the placement of the fabric. You must coordinate the blocks so that the fabrics from top to bottom and side to side match from one block to the next block as shown in the photo on page 59 and the quilt assembly diagram at right.

Assembling the Quilt Top

1. Lay out the blocks in four rows of three blocks each as shown in the quilt assembly diagram. Join the blocks into rows. Press the seam allowances in opposite directions from row to row. Sew the rows together and press the seam allowances in one direction. The quilt top should measure 14" x 18½".

2. Sew the white- or cream-solid 18½"-long strips to the left and right sides of the quilt top. Sew the white- or cream-solid 20"-long strips to the top and bottom of the quilt top. Press all seam allowances toward the border.

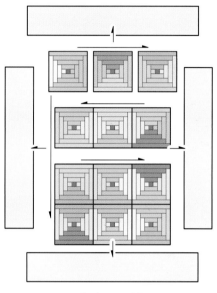

Quilt assembly

Preparing the Appliqués

For detailed instructions, refer to "Free-Motion Appliqué" on page 6. The patterns for the strawberries, strawberry tops, stem, leaf, flower, flower center, and bird are on page 63.

1. Trace one bird, one of each strawberry and strawberry top, one stem, 18 leaves, eight flowers, and eight flower centers onto the paper

4. Position and fuse the appliqué pieces on the border.

Stitching the Appliqués

Prepare your machine for free-motion appliqué as described in "Free-Motion Appliqué." Make two or three stitches at the beginning and end of each appliqué step before you lift the presser foot and needle and move to the next appliqué piece.

1. Free-motion stitch around each appliqué piece one time using light-colored thread.

2. Using six strands of embroidery floss and a backstitch, embroider green vines, an aqua bird wing, and a brown beak and legs. Stitch a brown French knot for the bird's eye.

3. Pull all the threads to the back of the border; knot and clip the threads. Press well.

side of the fusible web, leaving at least ½" between shapes. Cut out the fusible-web shapes, leaving ⅛" of web outside the traced line.

2. Place the fusible side of each shape on the wrong side of the corresponding fabric. As instructed on the pattern, place the bird on aqua solid; the strawberries on red prints; strawberry tops, stem, and leaves on green prints; flowers on a cream print; and flower centers on a yellow print. Using an iron, fuse the web to the fabric. Cut out the appliqué pieces on the traced lines and remove the paper backing.

3. Referring to the photo on page 59 for placement guidance, draw the embroidered vines onto the borders using a removable marking pen.

Quilting and Finishing

1. Layer the quilt top with batting and backing. Baste the layers together.

2. Quilt as desired. This quilt was stipple quilted using light-colored thread.

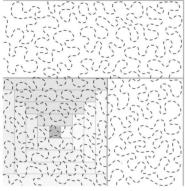

Quilting diagram

3. Trim the excess batting and backing even with the quilt top. Referring to "Binding" on page 77, use the red-floral 2½"-wide strips to make and attach the binding.

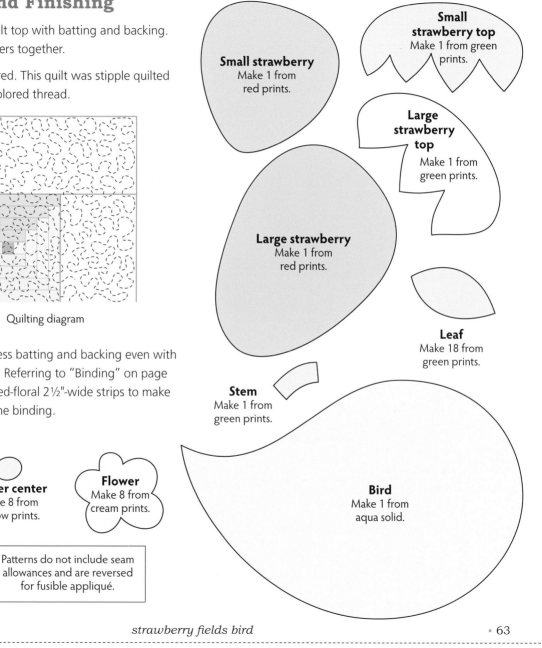

Small strawberry
Make 1 from
red prints.

Small strawberry top
Make 1 from green prints.

Large strawberry top
Make 1 from green prints.

Large strawberry
Make 1 from
red prints.

Leaf
Make 18 from
green prints.

Stem
Make 1 from
green prints.

Flower center
Make 8 from
yellow prints.

Flower
Make 8 from
cream prints.

Bird
Make 1 from
aqua solid.

Patterns do not include seam
allowances and are reversed
for fusible appliqué.

Birdbrain Ruffled Tote Bag

You have to have a super-cute tote bag when you visit the library or market. Using linen for the exterior and then adding a lining reinforces the bag, making it sturdy enough to hold books or groceries.

FINISHED SIZE: 14" x 14"

Materials

Yardage is based on 42"-wide fabric.

⅞ yard of natural-colored linen for bag body
½ yard of fabric for bag lining
⅓ yard of pink floral for ruffle and bird appliqué
Scrap, at least 2" x 3½", of mint solid for book appliqué
15" x 30" piece of mediumweight fusible interfacing
3½" x 7" piece of lightweight fusible web
Black thread for free-motion appliqué

Cutting

From the natural-colored linen, cut:
1 rectangle, 15" x 30"
2 strips, 4" x 42"

From the lining fabric, cut:
1 rectangle, 15" x 30"

From the pink floral, cut:
2 strips, 3" x 42"

Preparing the Appliqués

For detailed instructions, refer to "Free-Motion Appliqué" on page 6. The patterns for the bird and book are on page 69.

1. Place the interfacing fusible side down on the linen rectangle. Press until fused. Set aside.

2. Trace the bird and book patterns onto the paper side of the fusible web, leaving at least ½" between shapes. Cut out the fusible-web shapes, leaving ⅛" of web outside the traced line.

3. Place the fusible side of each shape onto the wrong side of the corresponding fabric. As instructed on the pattern, place the bird on the pink floral and the book on the mint solid. Using an iron, fuse the web to the fabric.

4. Cut out the appliqué pieces on the traced lines and remove the paper backing.

5. Fold the linen rectangle in half, wrong sides together and short ends aligned. Gently press the folded edge.

6. Place the bottom of the bird about 3½" up from the folded edge and the rounded part of the bird about 6½" from the left edge. Fuse in place.

7. Place the book about ½" from the rounded part of the bird. Fuse in place.

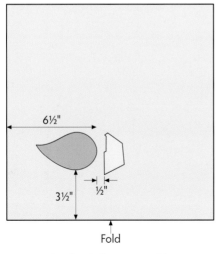

Appliqué placement guide

Stitching the Appliqués

Prepare your machine for free-motion appliqué as described in "Free-Motion Appliqué." Make two or three stitches at the beginning and end of each appliqué step before you lift the presser foot and needle and move to the next appliqué piece.

1. Starting along the round side of the bird, sew along the edge of the appliqué piece until you have gone around the bird completely.

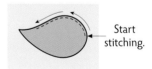

Start stitching.

2. Stitch a triangular-shaped beak onto the linen at the spot where you began.

3. Lift the presser foot and needle and move to the area of the bird where the eye should be; sew in a circular motion to make a small eye for the bird. Stitch a cute pair of glasses on the bird.

4. Move to the bottom or belly of the bird and stitch two parallel lines about ⅛" to ¼" apart to make the bird's legs.

5. Move to the book and stitch around the book two times. Stitch straight lines for the pages and spine of the book. Then stitch a word or two on the book for the title or author. I stitched the words *Jane Austen*.

6. Pull all the threads to the back of the linen; knot and clip the threads. Press well.

Assembling the Bag

Replace the free-motion foot with your general sewing presser foot.

1. Fold the appliquéd linen in half, right sides together, with the short ends aligned. Sew along both sides of the bag, using a ½" seam allowance.

2. Fold the lining in half, right sides together and short ends aligned. Sew along both sides of the lining, leaving a 4" opening for turning. Press the folded edge.

3. With the wrong sides out, fold one corner of the linen bag and align the side seam on top of the bottom crease to form a point; press flat. Measure 1" from the point and draw a line perpendicular to the seam. Sew along this line and trim ¼" from the stitched line to make a boxed corner. Repeat to box the other corner on the linen bag and both corners on the lining.

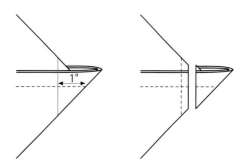

Making the Ruffle

1. Sew the pink-floral strips together end to end to make a long strip. Press the seam allowances open. Fold the strip in half lengthwise, wrong sides together.

2. Set your sewing machine to the longest stitch. Sew ⅛" from the raw edges of the strip, making sure to leave long tails of thread to gather the fabric.

3. Starting on one side of the strip, pull the top tail of thread to gather the ruffle, working the ruffles along the strip. You may find it helpful to pull the thread at the opposite end of the strip. Be careful not to break the thread. Gather the ruffles evenly until they fit around the top of the linen bag.

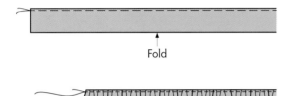

Fold

4. Align the raw edges of the ruffle with the top edge of the linen bag and pin in place. Baste the ruffle to the bag ⅛" from the raw edges.

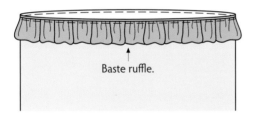

Baste ruffle.

Making the Straps

1. Fold the linen 4"-wide strips in half lengthwise, wrong sides together, and press the fold. Unfold, turn the raw edges of the strip to the center crease, refold on the center crease, and

then press the strip. Topstitch along each long side of the strap ⅛" from the edge. Repeat to make the second strap.

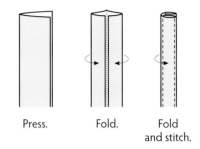

Press.   Fold.   Fold and stitch.

2. Place the straps over your shoulder to determine the desired length. Mark and cut the straps as needed.

3. Mark 4" from each side seam along the top edge of the linen bag. Place the raw edges of one strap about ½" beyond the raw edges of the bag. Pin the ends of the strap to the bag, aligning the outer edges of the strap with your 4" marks. Repeat with the remaining strap on the other side of the bag.

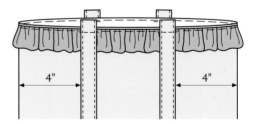

4"   4"

Finishing the Bag

1. With right sides together, place the lining inside the bag, sandwiching the straps between the layers. Align the raw edges and side seams; pin in place. Stitching through all the layers and using a ½" seam allowance, sew all the way around the top of the bag, backstitching over each strap.

2. Pull the bag through the gap in the lining seam. Gently poke out the corners. Sew the gap closed.

3. Push the lining into the bag. Pull up the ruffle and straps. Gently press the bag. Topstitch ⅛" from the top edge of the bag, beneath the ruffle.

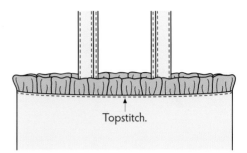

Topstitch.

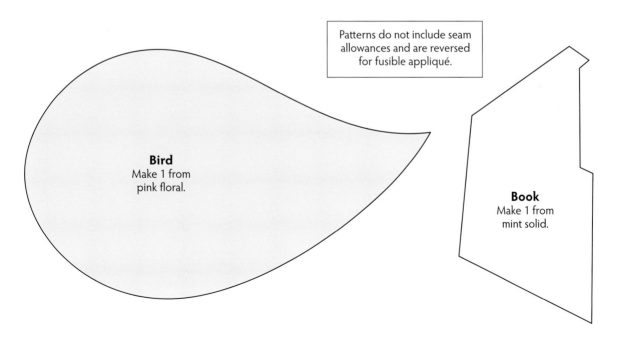

Patterns do not include seam allowances and are reversed for fusible appliqué.

Bird
Make 1 from
pink floral.

Book
Make 1 from
mint solid.

Mama Bird and Her Nest

I designed this charming little quilt to represent my children and me. It makes a thoughtful baby-shower or Mother's Day gift. You can easily change the number of eggs in the nest to represent each child in your family—or change the color scheme to match the baby's nursery.

FINISHED SIZE: 12½" x 16½"

Materials

Yardage is based on 42"-wide fabric.

⅜ yard of natural-colored linen for appliqué background

⅛ yard *total* of assorted blue prints for patchwork border and egg appliqués

⅛ yard *total* of assorted gray prints for patchwork border and bird appliqué

¼ yard of red print for binding

1 fat quarter (18" x 21") of fabric for backing

15" x 19" piece of batting

9½" x 13½" piece of lightweight fusible interfacing

6" x 6" square of lightweight fusible web

Black thread for free-motion appliqué

Cutting

From the natural-colored linen, cut:
1 rectangle, 9½" x 13½"

From the assorted blue prints, cut:
12 squares, 2½" x 2½"

From the assorted gray prints, cut:
12 squares, 2½" x 2½"

From the red print, cut:
2 strips, 2½" x 42"

Preparing the Appliqués

For detailed instructions, refer to "Free-Motion Appliqué" on page 6. The patterns for the bird and egg are on page 74.

5. Find the center of the linen rectangle by gently pressing the piece in half vertically and horizontally.

6. Place the bird in the center of the linen rectangle. Place the eggs about ⅝" to the left of the bird as shown. Fuse in place.

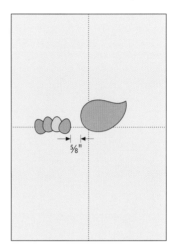

Appliqué placement guide

1. Place the interfacing fusible side down on the linen rectangle. Press until fused. Set aside.

2. Trace the bird and four eggs onto the paper side of the fusible web, leaving at least ½" between shapes. Note that I made four eggs to represent my children; you may want to make a different number of eggs to represent your family. Cut out the fusible-web shapes, leaving ⅛" of web outside the traced line.

3. Place each shape fusible side down onto the wrong side of the corresponding fabric. As instructed on the pattern, place the bird on a gray print and the eggs on the blue prints. Using an iron, fuse the web to the fabric.

4. Cut out the appliqué pieces on the traced lines and remove the paper backing.

Stitching the Appliqués

Prepare your machine for free-motion appliqué as described in "Free-Motion Appliqué." Make two or three stitches at the beginning and end of each appliqué step, before you lift the presser foot and needle and move to the next appliqué piece.

1. Starting along the round side of the bird, sew along the edge of the appliqué piece until you

sweet tweets

have gone around the bird completely one time. Sew around the bird one more time.

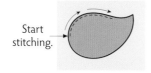

Start stitching.

2. Stitch a triangular-shaped beak onto the linen at the spot where you began. Sew over this two more times.

3. Lift the presser foot and needle and move to the area of the bird where the eye should be; sew in a circular motion to make a small eye for the bird.

4. Move to the bottom or belly of the bird and stitch two parallel lines about ⅛" to ¼" apart to make the bird's legs.

5. Move to the eggs. Stitch around each egg three times.

6. To make the nest, start in the center on one side of the eggs and stitch a line below the eggs, stopping at about the same point on the other side of the eggs. Sew back and forth four or five times, making sure your stitching lines touch the eggs and fill in the area below the eggs.

7. On the left edge of the linen, below the bird's legs and nest, start stitching the branch that the bird and nest rest on. Stitch toward the right of the linen, stopping about ½" beyond

the bird. Go back to the left side and then back to the right side, making sure that your stitching lines touch the bird's legs and nest. Stitch back and forth until the branch is the desired thickness.

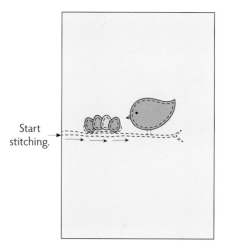

Start stitching.

8. Pull all the threads to the back of the linen background; knot and clip the threads.

9. Press well. Trim the appliquéd piece to measure 8½" x 12½", trimming equally on all sides.

Adding the Patchwork Border

Replace the free-motion foot with your general sewing presser foot.

1. Arrange the blue and gray squares in a pleasing manner around the appliquéd piece as shown in the photo on page 71.

2. Sew four squares together to make the top border. Press the seam allowances in one direction. Repeat to make the bottom border. Sew the borders to the top and bottom of the appliquéd piece. Press the seam allowances toward the borders.

3. Sew eight squares together to make a side border. Press the seam allowances in the directions indicated. Repeat to make a second side border. Sew these borders to the left and right sides of the appliquéd piece. Press the seam allowances toward the borders.

Quilting and Finishing

1. Layer the quilt top with batting and backing. Baste the layers together.

2. Quilt as desired. This quilt was outline quilted ⅛" from the edge of the patchwork with natural-colored thread.

3. Trim the excess batting and backing even with the quilt top. Referring to "Binding" on page 77, use the red 2½"-wide strips to make and attach the binding.

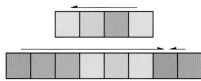

Make 2 of each.

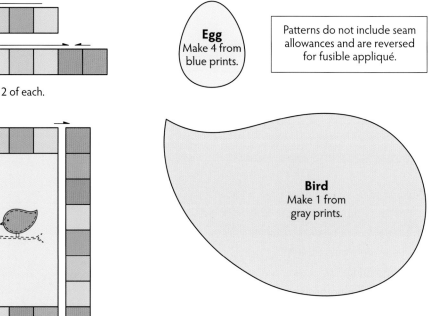

Egg
Make 4 from blue prints.

Patterns do not include seam allowances and are reversed for fusible appliqué.

Bird
Make 1 from gray prints.

Quiltmaking Basics

If you're new to quilting, there are many quilting books that offer all the info you'll need. You can also visit ShopMartingale.com/HowtoQuilt to download free how-to guides that you can save, print, and refer to as often as you need. In this section, I'll briefly cover a few quiltmaking basics.

Tools and Supplies

In addition to the appliqué supplies mentioned on page 6, you'll need the following tools and supplies to complete the projects in this book.

- Rotary cutter, self-healing cutting mat (18" x 24"), and acrylic ruler (6" x 24")
- Scissors
- Sewing machine
- Seam ripper
- Iron
- Light-colored 50-weight thread for piecing
- Needles for hand and machine sewing
- Hera marker for marking quilting lines
- Curved safety pins for basting
- Cotton batting
- Open-toe darning or free-motion presser foot
- Walking foot for quilting and attaching binding

Rotary Cutting

Accurate piecing begins with accurately cut shapes. It's essential to cut strips at an exact right angle to the folded edge of the fabric.

1. Iron the fabric; then fold it with wrong sides together and opposite selvages aligned. Lay the fabric on the cutting mat with the fold toward you. The raw edges may be uneven.

2. Straighten one end of the fabric by positioning a ruler along the right edge of the fabric, with a horizontal line of the ruler aligned with the fold and the right cutting edge just inside all the layers of the fabric. Starting at the fold, rotary cut along the right edge of the ruler and remove the waste strip.

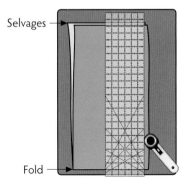

Align a horizontal mark on the ruler with the fold. Cut along the edge of the ruler.

3. Rotate the mat 180°, being careful that the fabric does not shift. To cut a strip, align the desired strip width on the ruler with the cut edge of the fabric, and carefully cut a strip.

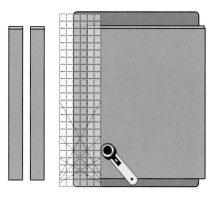

4. To cut squares and rectangles, cut a strip the desired width and carefully remove the selvage ends by making a cleanup cut. Align the desired measurement on the ruler with the left edge of the strip and cut a square or rectangle. Continue cutting until you have the required number of pieces.

Machine Piecing

I use a good-quality light-colored 100% cotton thread for piecing. For appliqué, I use either black or natural-colored thread. For quilting, the color of thread depends on the project, and I use either a 50-weight or 40-weight thread. The lower the number, the heavier the thread. I prefer a universal size 80/12 sewing-machine needle, but I keep a variety of needle sizes on hand. Many issues with thread tension can be solved with just the right needle. The best sewing advice I ever received was to change my needle often and oil my machine after about eight hours of sewing.

Quilts are much easier to sew if you use an accurate ¼" seam allowance. Even if you use a ¼" presser foot, you may find that your seam allowances are slightly wider or narrower than a true ¼". Check your seam allowance for accuracy when starting a new project.

When possible, I use assembly-line piecing, feeding pieces through the machine one after the other and stopping to cut the thread only when an entire group is sewn. This is called chain piecing.

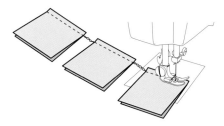

After stitching the seams, press the pieces just as they came out of your sewing machine—with right sides still together. Pressing sets the seam, making the stitching nice and flat so that the thread takes up less bulk once you press the pieces open. With the darker patch on top, use the tip of your iron to open up the pieces, and then press the seam flat from the right side. This way, the seam allowances will automatically be facing the dark fabric. Use a dry iron and spray mist the pieces with water if needed.

Right side of fabric

When sewing one unit to another, press seam allowances that must match in opposite directions. The opposing seam allowances hold the seams in place and evenly distribute the fabric bulk. Plan pressing to take advantage of opposing seams.

Opposing seams

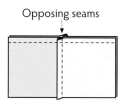

Basting and Quilting

Press the quilt top and backing to remove wrinkles. Then spread the backing wrong side up on a flat, clean surface. Anchor the backing with masking tape, taking care not to stretch the fabric. Center the batting over the backing, smoothing out any wrinkles. Center the quilt top, right side up, over the batting, again smoothing out any wrinkles. Baste the layers with curved safety pins, pinning about 4" apart. Remove the tape.

Quilting is what holds the layers of fabric and batting together. To quilt on your home sewing machine, I recommend using two different types of presser feet. To quilt straight lines, use a walking foot. It helps move the layers evenly through the machine, which prevents bunching and pulling. If you want to free-motion quilt, you'll need to use a free-motion or darning foot, which may be open or a fully-closed round foot. A free-motion foot allows you to freely move the fabric in various directions to create stippling and many other designs, hence the name *free-motion quilting*.

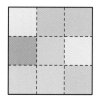

Quilting in the ditch   Straight-line quilting

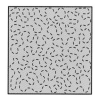

Stippling

Binding

After quilting, use a cutting mat, ruler, and rotary cutter to trim the batting and backing so the edges are even with the quilt top. Most of the projects in this book use a double-fold binding made with 2½"-wide strips. Cut the required number of strips as instructed for the project.

1. Place two strips at right angles, right sides together. Draw a diagonal line on the top strip and stitch along the marked line. Trim the seam allowances to ¼" and press them open. Add the remaining strips in the same manner to make one long strip.

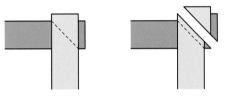

Joining strips

Press seam allowances open.

2. Press the strip in half lengthwise, wrong sides together.

3. Starting in the middle of one side, place an end of the binding strip on the right side of the quilt, aligning the raw edges of the binding strip with the quilt-top edge. Using a walking foot and a ¼" seam allowance, begin stitching about 6" from the start of the binding. Stop stitching ¼" from the first corner and backstitch. Remove the quilt from the machine.

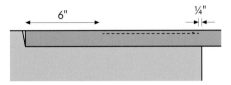

4. Fold the binding straight up so that the fold creates a 45° angle. Fold the binding back down onto itself, even with the raw edge of the quilt top. Begin stitching at the fold with a backstitch. Continue sewing along the edge of the quilt top; stop ¼" from the next corner.

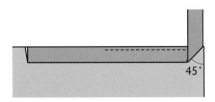

5. Repeat the process on the remaining edges and corners of the quilt.

6. Stop stitching 8" to 10" from the starting end of the binding strip. Remove the quilt from the

sweet tweets

machine. To join the binding ends, place the quilt on a flat surface and overlap the beginning and ending binding tails. Trim the tails so they overlap exactly 2½", or the same width as your binding strips.

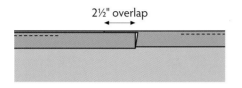

2½" overlap

7. Unfold the binding ends and place them right sides together, perpendicular to one another; pin. Draw a diagonal line from corner to corner, and then stitch on the drawn line. Make sure the binding is the correct length to fit your quilt and that the seam was sewn in the correct direction. When satisfied, trim the excess corner fabric, leaving a ¼" seam allowance. Press the seam allowances open.

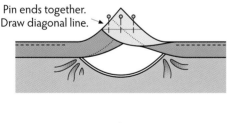

Pin ends together.
Draw diagonal line.

8. Refold the binding, position it along the quilt, and finish stitching it in place.

9. Fold the binding over the raw edges to the quilt back, with the folded edge covering the row of machine stitching. Hand stitch the binding in place. When you reach a corner, sew just beyond the machine-stitched corner. Fold the next side to form a mitered corner. Tack the miter in place, and continue stitching.

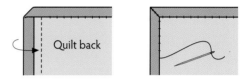

Quilt back

Alternate Binding Method

For some of the projects, I used an alternate method of binding that's faster and stronger than hand binding. For this method, I sew the binding to the back of the quilt, instead of the front, in the same manner as described here in "Binding." Then I fold the binding to the front of the quilt and edgestitch by machine along the fold of the binding.

Acknowledgments

With a grateful and humble heart I'd like to thank many people because you're all very special to me, and I wouldn't be writing this book without you:

First, above all, I thank God my creator, for continually extending grace and mercy to me. You've blessed me with a beautiful life.

My husband and kids, for supporting and encouraging my obsession with fabric, sewing, quilting, and in writing this book. Love you more!

My mom, for passing down her thrifty gene and through example teaching me to make do and do it myself as early as I can remember. You're a constant source of encouragement. I love you!

My dad, for always letting me play with the prismacolors. I love you and miss you terribly. I wish you could see this!

My mother-in-law, for giving me my first real working sewing machine and showing me how to use it. Thank you for all of your encouragement since I began sewing.

A huge thank-you to Karen Burns, Cathy Reitan, Nancy Mahoney, Marcy Heffernan, Adrienne Smitke, and all the people at Martingale who helped to make this book. It's truly a dream come true.

A special thank-you to all of my friends in the quilt community. You're some of the most creative and generous people I've ever known. I have met so many awesome people through my blog and quilting, and I really wouldn't have half as much fun sewing without all of you!

About the Author

ERIN COX is a quilter and homemaker. She lives in the rural Appalachian Mountains of West Virginia. Her love for quilting started 13 years ago while she was living in Lancaster County, Pennsylvania, where she was surrounded by beautiful Amish and Mennonite quilts. After sewing her first Churn Dash block, she was hooked. Quilting has been a part of her everyday life ever since. Please visit Erin at www.WhyNotSew.blogspot.com